101 Best Gluten-Free Foods

Health Research Staff

Millwood Media LLC
Melrose, FL

101 BEST GLUTEN-FREE FOODS
Health Research Staff

Published by:
Millwood Media LLC
PO Box 1220
Melrose, FL 32666 USA
www.MillwoodMediaEpub.com

Copyright © 2011-2012 by Millwood Media LLC

ISBN 13 : 978-1-937918-45-3

Health Disclaimer

Table of Contents

Introduction vii

Almond Butter...........................1
Almond Flour 1
Almonds 3
Apples.......................................3
Apricots....................................4
Asparagus 4
Avocados 5
Bananas 5
Beets...7
Bell Peppers.............................7
Black Beans 8
Blackberries 8
Blueberries 9
Beef 10
Broccoli 10
Brussels Sprouts 11
Buckwheat 11
Cabbage 13
Cantaloupe 13
Cashews..................................14
Carrots 14
Cauliflower 16
Celery 16
Cheese 17
Cherries..................................17
Chick Peas 18

Chicken 18
Cod 19
Collard Greens 19
Corn 20
Corn Meal 20
Coffee 21
Cucumbers 21
Eggplant 22
Fennel................................. 23
Figs 23
Flaxseeds 24
Garlic 24
Grapefruit 25
Grapes 27
Greek Yogurt 27
Green Beans 28
Green Peas........................... 28
Green Tea 29
Halibut 30
Kale 30
Kidney Beans 31
Kiwifruit.............................. 31
Leeks 33
Lentils 33
Lemons................................ 34
Lima Beans 35
Mangoes 35
Millet.................................. 36

Miso 36
Mushrooms 37
Mustard Greens 38
Navy Beans 39
Olives 40
Olive Oil 41
Onions 43
Oranges 44
Papaya 45
Peanuts 46
Pears 46
Peas 47
Pineapple 47
Pinto Beans 49
Plums 49
Pork 50
Potatoes 51
Pumpkin Seeds 52
Quinoa 53
Raisins 54
Raspberries 55
Rice 56
Rice Flour 56
Romaine Lettuce 57
Salmon 58
Sardines 59
Scallops 60
Sesame Seeds 61

Shrimp 62
Spinach 64
Strawberries 65
Soy Flour 66
Soybeans 67
Squash 68
Sunflower seeds 69
Swiss Chard 69
Sweet Potato 70
Tofu 70
Tomatoes 71
Tuna 71
Turkey 72
Turnip Greens 72
Venison 73
Walnuts 73
Watermelon 74
Yams 74
Zucchini 75

Handy List for Shopping for the
101 Best Gluten-Free Foods 76

Traveling With Celiac Disease ... 78

Introduction

Welcome to your guide to gluten-free foods. Gluten intolerance is a problem that more and more people are becoming aware of because an increasing number of people are being impacted by this problem.

While there are some people who are simply sensitive to gluten and feel much better eating a gluten-free diet, there are those who are gluten intolerant and must immediately cut all gluten out of their diet if they are to maintain good health.

So what is gluten intolerance anyway?

Gluten is a particular type of protein composite that is found in wheat, rye, as well as barley that certain individuals are unable to digest properly. When they eat foods containing this gluten protein composite, their body triggers the immune system to react and they start producing antibodies in defense.

Over time, these antibodies will begin to wear down the microscopic hairs that line the walls of the intestine that are used to help absorb nutrients from the foods that you are eating.

As these 'villi', as they're referred to, are destroyed, you'll lose the ability to absorb all the nutrients that you should and slowly start to experience severe nutritional deficiencies because of it.

Some of the symptoms that are associated with gluten intolerance include:

- *Abdominal distension*

- *Abdominal pain and cramping*

- *Diarrhea and/or constipation*

- *Bloating*

- *Depression*

- *Fatigue*

- *Headaches*

- *Hypoglycemia*

- *As well as many diseases and conditions associated with nutritional deficiencies*

Individuals who are suffering from this condition are advised to adopt a diet that is completely free of gluten rich foods as this will then keep these negative side effects to a minimum.

What's also important to keep in mind is the fact that even those who aren't suffering from gluten intolerance can benefit from a gluten-free diet plan.

Many of the gluten-rich foods that we consume on an everyday basis are going to cause our blood sugar levels to increase and then crash dramatically, which can begin to wear out the insulin system as well. Over time, this could then lead to the development of diabetes, placing you further into a state of negative health.

By focusing on a gluten-free diet plan, you'll maintain a much healthier intake of foods and eat those that support a healthy body weight, reduce inflammation, and go a long way towards preventing the development of disease.

So now that you have a basic understanding of what gluten intolerance is, let's go over the main gluten-free foods that you should be eating.

Remember to eat an even distribution from this list of protein rich foods, carbohydrate rich foods, and healthy fat rich foods for best results.

* * * * *

Attention All Eagle Eyes: We've had a number of people proof this book before we released it to you, but there is a chance you might spot something that was missed. If you find a typo or other obvious error please send it to us. And if you're the first one to report it, we'll send you a free gift! Send to: **millwoodmedia@gmail.com**

* * * * *

101 Best Gluten-Free Foods

1. Almond Butter

For those who prefer to smear their healthy fats, almond butter is an excellent selection. Almond butter tastes great on apples, bananas, or added into a smoothie and will offer very similar health benefits as whole almonds do. Best of all, almond butter contains less sugar than peanut butter does, making this a healthier pick for your diet plan.

2. Almond Flour

If you're doing some baking, almond flour might be an option for you to consider. On a gluten-free diet wheat based flour will be out of the question, so almond flour can stand in as a suitable replacement in many recipes. Almond flour will contain many of the same health benefits as almond would.

3. Almonds

If you want to minimize your hunger, almonds are a great food to turn to. Chock full of healthy fats, this food will keep your blood sugar levels stable so that you can feel energized all day long. This nut can also help to control the amount of insulin secretion experienced, as found by a study in the Metabolism Journal. Almonds are a terrific source of manganese, vitamin E, magnesium, tryptophan, as well as copper and will help to promote good heart health as well.

4. Apples

One of the top fruits to eat to banish hunger quickly is the apple. Apples contain a form of fiber known as pectin, which works especially hard to keep your appetite down. Apples also are excellent for regulating blood sugar levels, which anyone using a gluten-free diet can benefit from. This fruit will also help to promote healthy digestion, so will ensure that you reap all the nutritional benefits from the foods that you eat.

5. Apricots

Apricots are a standout source of vitamin A as well as vitamin C, two nutrients that will help to protect you from heart disease. In addition to this, apricots are excellent for fending off free radical damage, which could lead to the development of cancer. Apricots are also high in dietary fiber, which will help to calm your hunger pains.

6. Asparagus

Asparagus really is a nutrient powerhouse, being rich in vitamin K, C, A, B vitamins, folate, tryptophan, manganese, as well as copper. This vegetable also contains a small amount of iron, so will be very beneficial for helping to keep your energy levels up. At just 43 calories per cup, it's an easy add into any diet plan. The saponins found in asparagus will help to fend off cancer and inflammation, which are two further reasons to add this to your meal plan.

7. Avocados

The avocado is one fruit that is rare from the rest in that they contain a high amount of healthy fats that will help to provide long-term energy and keep your hormone levels healthy. In addition to this, they also offer a good dose of vitamin K, dietary fiber, potassium, folate, and vitamin B6. This is a higher calorie food however at 235 calories per cup, so make sure that you keep your serving size in check. Finally, as stated in the Journal of Ethnopharmacology, those consuming diets rich in avocados may experience reduced blood pressure as a result of it.

8. Bananas

The stand-out nutrient that's found in bananas is vitamin B6, as they offer 35% of your daily quota. Bananas are also rich in potassium, which is important for promoting strong muscular contractions. In addition to that, bananas are very easy on the digestive tract, so good to eat for those who have sensitive systems. This food offers good protection from cardiovascular disease and will also help assist the elimination process.

9. Beets

One vegetable that's very often forgotten about, beets also offer a number of nutrients to be aware of. This food is very high in phytonutrients referred to as betalains, which can provide antioxidant and anti-inflammatory support. They're a good source of folate, manganese, potassium, as well as vitamin C and magnesium, and will also provide some iron as well. Beets also assist with detoxifying the body, so by adding them regularly you can ensure that you feel your best on a day to day basis.

10. Bell Peppers

Not hard to spot in the supermarket, the brightly colored bell pepper offers clear nutritional benefits. This food is extremely high in vitamin C and A, which are important for protecting the body against free radicals and offering antioxidant support. For top antioxidant protection, go with green peppers which offer slightly higher levels of protection against yellow, orange, and red peppers, as noted in the Journal of Food Science. In addition to this, they also contain vitamin B6, vitamin K, folate, potassium, and vitamin B1, all necessary to maintain high energy levels and support proper growth and development.

11. Black Beans

Most people know beans for their high fiber content, but this food has so much more to offer than just that. Black beans are a powerful source of molybdenum, folate, tryptophan, manganese, as well as vitamin B1 and will also provide some iron as well. For anyone who is a vegetarian and often has difficulty obtaining enough iron in their diet, this is a perfect food to be eating. Black beans will also help to support a healthy digestive track.

12. Blackberries

Many people often opt for other berries over blackberries, but these really should not be forgotten. Blackberries are a powerful source of antioxidants that will help to protect against cancer and other diseases. In addition to this, they'll also help to provide you with a potent dose of fiber, making it easier to reach your daily needs. Blackberries work great in so many different dishes, so make sure you give them some consideration at your next meal.

13. Blueberries

One berry that has been known to provide excellent brain benefits, blueberries are very high in antioxidant content and will provide you with a powerful source of vitamin C. Blueberries offer clear cardiovascular benefits and will help to protect the lining of the blood vessel walls around the heart. In addition to that, blueberries also offer clear brain benefits, so anyone who wants to maintain a sound mind will want to include this food in their daily diet.

14. Beef

One powerful source of protein that you should consider adding to your diet is lean beef. Beef is especially healthy if you purchase grass fed varieties as then it will also be high in healthy omega fats. Beef is going to easily help you meet your protein needs and will supply you with a good dose of iron as well, necessary for maintaining high energy levels. Beef is also rich in zinc and selenium, so this will further help to promote overall health and help to build muscle as well.

15. Broccoli

A vegetable that earns top marks for the nutrition that it offers is broccoli. Broccoli is great for lowering your cholesterol level and helping to assist with the detoxification process. In addition to that, broccoli also contains a high dose of vitamin C, vitamin K, vitamin A, folate, dietary fiber, potassium, vitamin B 2 and 6 as well as magnesium. For anyone who is suffering from inflammatory conditions, broccoli can also help you gain control over those as well.

16. Brussels Sprouts

A vegetable that is often overlooked due to its taste, Brussels sprouts are going to go a long way to lower your cholesterol levels while helping to provide strong detoxification to your body. This vegetable will also help to support a healthy digestive system and can help to fend off inflammation. For those who are concerned about diabetes, metabolic syndrome, or crohn's disease, this is one vegetable that you should make sure you are eating enough of.

17. Buckwheat

Since you are unable to eat many of the complex wheat derived food sources on your gluten free diet, buckwheat is an excellent stand in. This food is rich in manganese, tryptophan, and will also help to provide clear cardiovascular health benefits. Buckwheat is great for promoting good blood glucose control as well, so will help anyone who suffers from blood sugar highs and lows throughout the day.

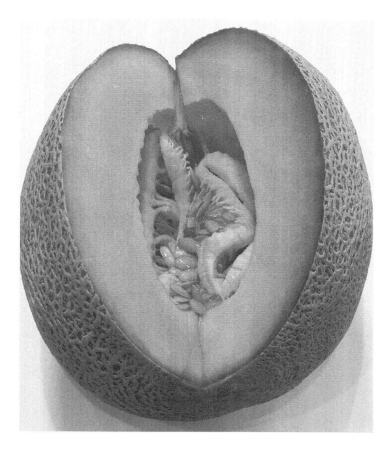

18. Cabbage

Whether you choose to eat green or red cabbage, this is one vegetable that will provide numerous health benefits. Cabbage is high in vitamin K, C, the B vitamins, vitamin A, folate, omega fatty acids, calcium, and potassium. Essentially, it's like its own multi-vitamin. Cabbage is also low in calories at just 33 per cup, so perfect for those watching their weight. The antioxidant support this food provides will help to ward off cancer as well as many other diseases.

19. Cantaloupe

One of the most potent nutrients found in the cantaloupe is vitamin A, making this an excellent fruit for offering strong anti-oxidant protection. In addition to this, it also supplies you with over 100% of your daily needs for vitamin C and provides potassium, folate, and vitamin B6 as well. This fruit will help to enhance your lung health and also support good eyesight.

20. Cashews

Cashews are a nut high in healthy fats and one that will also provide you with copper, magnesium, tryptophan, and phosphorus. This nut will provide strong antioxidant protection as well and help to support healthy bones and blood vessels. In addition to this, it will also offer solid heart health benefits being that it is so high in healthy fats, as mentioned in a study performed by The Pennsylvania State University.

21. Carrots

For healthy eyes, carrots are a top pick. This vegetable provides over 600% of your vitamin A needs with just a one cup serving, so you will not need to worry about getting your needs met with it in your diet. In addition to that, it also provides vitamin K, vitamin C, potassium, vitamin B6, vitamin B1, vitamin B3 as well as magnesium, all nutrients that will support high energy levels. With a sweet taste that most people enjoy, this is a perfect add to any gluten-free diet.

22. Cauliflower

Known as a cruciferous vegetable, cauliflower is another great addition to your diet plan. This vegetable is rich in vitamin C and vitamin K, and will also provide you with a folate and dietary fiber content. It also offers some vitamin B6, tryptophan, omega 3 fatty acids as well as manganese, contributing over 10% of your total daily requirements for each of these nutrients. Rated low on the GI index, this vegetable will easily help you control your blood sugar level.

23. Celery

If you're someone who is suffering from high blood pressure, celery is the vegetable that you'll want to be turning to. Celery has strong blood pressure lowering benefits and is also high in vitamin C, making it excellent for promoting a strong immune system. Celery can also help to reduce the level of cholesterol in the body, and will act as a diuretic as well. Finally, celery is great for helping to ward against cancer.

24. Cheese

For those of you who aren't drinking a lot of milk in your everyday diet plan, cheese is an excellent way to meet your calcium needs and to get a good dose of protein as well. Be sure to choose lower fat varieties of cheese as often as possible as these will be the ones that contain the least amount of saturated fat. The high amount of calcium in cheese will go a long way towards promoting strong bones and keeping your muscles relaxed.

25. Cherries

One sweet fruit that many people should be eating more of in their daily diet is cherries. Cherries are ranked in very low on the GI index scale so will have minimal impact on your blood sugar levels. In addition to that, cherries have strong antioxidant protection, so will help to ward of diseases such as cancer, diabetes, and heart disease. Finally, cherries are also a potent source of beta carotene, vitamin C, magnesium, iron, fiber, and folate.

26. Chick Peas

An excellent source of fiber to include in your diet plan that is gluten-free and an excellent source of carbohydrates are chick peas. Chick peas are very high in molybdenum, manganese, folate, dietary fiber, tryptophan, copper, as well as phosphorus, and will contain some iron as well. They do contain 268 calories per cup so will contribute more calories than some other foods, making portion control vitally important.

27. Chicken

If you're looking for a good way to get some protein into your day, chicken is the food to add. Chicken is very rich in tryptophan, vitamin B3, selenium, vitamin B6, as well as phosphorus and will support and active lifestyle. Chicken is a very low fat source of protein, making it ideal for those watching their weight and using a gluten-free diet plan.

28. Cod

Cod is one of the lowest fat sources of protein, being almost entirely fat free and is highly versatile in the different ways in which you can prepare it. Cod is very rich in tryptophan, contains a good dose of selenium, is high in vitamin the B vitamins which are imperative to promote good energy levels, and contains a healthy dose of vitamin D as well. Consuming cod on a regular basis can help to promote good cardiovascular health and support proper muscle function.

29. Collard Greens

Collard greens are a great cruciferous vegetable to be eating if you're worried about your current cholesterol levels as it'll help bring your levels down. In addition to that, this vegetable also offers strong protection against cancer and provides you with a good dose of vitamin K, A, and C. Collard greens are rich in manganese, folate, calcium, as well as dietary fiber, and will help to decrease the inflammation in the body.

30. Corn

Corn is a vegetable that is more starch-based compared to many other lower calorie vegetables, so great for those who are gluten free diets to help maintain their energy levels. Corn has extremely high antioxidant benefits, so will help to ward off cancer and other forms of disease. In addition to this, corn supports a healthy digestive system and can help regulate your blood sugar levels so you experience less highs and lows throughout the day.

31. Corn Meal

Corn meal is another good substitute for those who are using a gluten-free diet to help keep their carbohydrate intake up along with their energy levels stable. Per one cup serving of raw cornmeal you'll be getting 93.8 grams of carbs with almost 9 grams of fiber. The fat content is low at just 4.4 grams with only 0.6 of those coming from saturated sources. Corn meal is also entirely sugar free, so won't cause a blood sugar spike or crash like some other carbs may.

32. Coffee

Coffee, while not considered a 'food' per se, is another thing that can be added to gluten-free diets. Coffee can help to increase attention and alertness, so for those benefits, many people do use it throughout the day. In addition to this, a study published in the Diabetes Care Journal indicated that habitual coffee intake can lower the risk of type 2 diabetes.

33. Cucumbers

One of the vegetables that has the highest level of water is cucumbers, which will quickly help hydrate the body without adding hardly any calories at all. Cucumbers are high in vitamin C, vitamin A, potassium, manganese, folate, as well as dietary fiber and contain a number of flavonoids and lignans to help protect against free radicals. Add these to a salad to reap their health benefits.

34. Eggplant

Eggplant is a vegetable that many people often overlook in their diets but may want to reconsider due to all the many different health benefits it has to offer. Eggplants are rated high as one of the top 'brain foods' that you could be eating as they can protect against free radical scavengers and make sure nutrients are reaching the brain. In addition to this, eggplants are also good for supporting your cardiovascular system as they'll help to keep your blood cholesterol levels in check and help to improve blood flow to and from the heart.

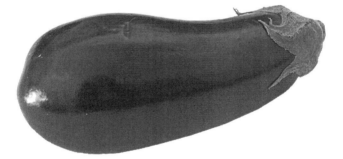

35. Fennel

Another vegetable that few people consider adding to their diet on a regular basis is fennel. Fennel offers a slightly sweet taste to your dishes, so will be a welcomed change of pace for most people. Fennel is a rich source of vitamin C, dietary fiber, potassium, manganese, folate, as well as phosphorus, and will also supply a small amount of iron and calcium as well. Fennel is a great food for boosting your immune system so can help prevent you from feeling run down.

36. Figs

Figs are the next gluten-free food to consider adding to your diet. These are a calorie dense food coming in at 167 calories per 8 oz serving, so compared with other fruit, you do want to watch your serving size. Figs can help to bring down your overall blood pressure level and are also a potent source of dietary fiber. This is going to ensure that you're able to effectively manage your blood sugar levels throughout the day, preventing highs and lows. Finally, figs can help promote strong and dense bone tissue due to their elevated calcium content.

37. Flaxseeds

To help meet your daily quota of omega fats, turn to flaxseeds. Flaxseeds are not only high in essential fatty acids, but they're also a rich source of fiber as well. This combination makes them ideal for helping to keep you satisfied between meals. The omega fats found in flaxseeds will also help to protect against insulin resistance and keep your brain healthy. Finally, a study published in the European Journal of Clinical Nutrition noted that flaxseed consumption can help to lower blood pressure.

38. Garlic

One interesting thing to note about garlic, one of the most flavorful ingredients that you could add to your dishes is that it can help to promote iron absorption. For anyone who is concerned about iron deficiency anemia, this is definitely a benefit not to overlook. In addition to that, garlic can also help to help promote a healthy heart as well as provide antibacterial and antiviral benefits. Finally, garlic can also offer mild cancer protection, so adding it to your meals is well worth the effort.

39. Grapefruit

Commonly thought of when referring to the 'grapefruit' diet, this low calorie fruit is a very rich source of vitamin C, so will help to promote a strong immune system. In addition to this, grapefruit also contains a high amount of lycopene, so will help to promote protection against free radical damage to your cells. Finally, grapefruit can help to lower your overall cholesterol levels, providing clear heart health rewards for those who consume it regularly. Whether you're enjoying red or white grapefruit, you'll still reap these same benefits.

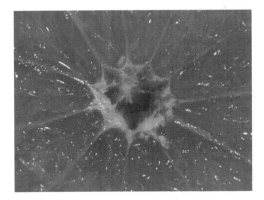

40. Grapes

The fruit that gives wine its health benefits, grapes are a sweet treat that's generally quite low in calories as well. They rate in low on the glycemic index scale and will help you better manage your insulin response. Grapes are incredibly rich in flavanols and carotenoids, two forms of antioxidants that will keep you healthy. In addition to this, grapes can help to reduce the signs of aging and enhance longevity as well. Finally, grapes have a positive impact on brain health. Freeze some for a cold treat on a hot day.

41. Greek Yogurt

Yogurt is another of the healthiest foods that you could be adding to your diet and when you choose Greek yogurt, it gets that much healthier. Greek yogurt is incredibly low in sugar, but yet very high in protein, so will go a long way towards helping you meet your daily nutritional requirement while keeping your hunger low. It's also going to help to provide calcium to support strong bones, which will improve the chances that you can maintain your activity level for a long time to come.

42. Green Beans

Green beans another relatively low calorie food, so ideal for those who are on fat loss diet plans. With just 43 calories per cup, they can easily fit in with any diet plan. They're also a rich source of vitamin K, vitamin C, vitamin A, potassium, folate, tryptophan, as well as iron, amongst many other nutrients. Green beans will provide you with good antioxidant support and will also help to keep your heart healthy as well.

43. Green Peas

Green peas are another green food to eat on your gluten-free diet. Green peas are rich in vitamin K, manganese, vitamin C, as well as fiber and will provide a number of B vitamins. They will help to support a healthy metabolism and energy production level, so you feel your best all day long. Since many people on gluten-free diets may fall short with their carbohydrate intake, this is a good food to consume to help avoid that.

44. Green Tea

Another beverage that's a must have as you go about your diet plan is green tea. Green tea is loaded with antioxidants that can help to protect you against free radical damage and will also contain a small dose of caffeine as well, which will help to provide a nice burst of energy when you need it. One added benefit of green tea that often does go overlooked is also the fact that it can help to boost your metabolic rate as well, so for anyone looking for fat loss, it can be a very powerful tool in your quest for results. A study published by the American Journal of Clinical Nutrition noted that green tea consumption produced a significant increase in the 24 hour metabolic rate compared to a placebo.

45. Halibut

The next protein source that's great for gluten-free diets is halibut. Halibut is rich in tryptophan, selenium, as well as vitamin B3 and will provide you with a good dose of omega 3 fatty acids as well. These fats are especially important for good heart and brain health, and are a nutrient that the body cannot make on its own. Halibut is also rich in magnesium, which will help to promote strong blood vessels and veins around the heart.

46. Kale

Adding steamed kale to your diet plan is one of the best ways to promote a lower level of cholesterol in the body and decrease your risk for cancer. In addition to that, it's also high in vitamin K, vitamin A, as well as vitamin C, so will offer strong immune system support as well as antioxidant protection. Kale also has detoxifying effects in the body as well, so can help you feel healthier on a regular basis when included in your diet regularly. With seven grams of fiber per 100 calories, it's also considered a high fiber food.

47. Kidney Beans

Kidney beans are another high fiber food to include in your diet that are gluten free and will also offer a good dose of protein as well as complex carbohydrates. For those leading a very active lifestyle, this food is wonderful for maintaining those activity levels and achieving a better overall recovery rate. Kidney beans will also help to lower your risk of heart attacks through their high folate, magnesium, and fiber levels and will help to stabilize your blood sugar levels as well. Finally, kidney beans are also rich in iron, which is imperative for maintaining your energy levels.

48. Kiwifruit

One fruit that's a very potent source of vitamin C is kiwifruit. These small fruits contain just 46 calories and will also pack in some fiber, potassium, copper, and magnesium. Kiwi's are rich in phytonutrients that will help to protect your DNA, ensuring proper cell replication takes place as it should. In addition to that, kiwi's will also help to enhance your blood sugar control and promote a healthier colon as well. Those who are suffering asthma will especially want to consider adding kiwi's to their diet as this fruit can help to reduce the symptoms associated with this condition.

49. Leeks

A great addition to any meal you're preparing, leeks contain flavonoids that can help to improve your health and reduce your risk of disease. They contain a small dose of manganese, vitamin C, iron, and folate, and will also boost your cardiovascular system as well. Try sautéing them in some lemon juice for added flavor.

50. Lentils

Lentils are a great food for anyone who struggles to get in enough protein to eat as they'll be a good non-meat source of this nutrient. In addition to that, they also supply you with folate, dietary fiber, tryptophan, manganese, iron, as well as phosphorus, so will help to support high energy levels and muscle synthesis. The fiber found in lentils is both soluble fiber as well as insoluble fiber, so these will not only help to keep your bowel movements regular, but also help to add bulk to the diet so you're not as hungry as you go about your day. Finally, anyone who is a vegetarian will be at risk for low levels of iron and lentils can help to provide this nutrient to prevent deficiency. For a better blood glucose response to lentil consumption, dry your lentils in the oven at 250 degrees for 12 hours after cooking, as noted in the American Journal of Clinical Nutrition.

51. Lemons

A tart food that works great with many dishes you cook, lemons do contain some powerful health benefits to know about. This gluten-free food is very high in vitamin C and also supplies some antioxidant and antibiotic effects to your body. Eating lemons on a regular basis can help to stop cell division in many cancer cell lines, so can help ward off the development of this disease. Lemons can also help to protect against the development of rheumatoid arthritis, so if anyone in your family impacted by this condition, you'll want to add more lemons to your daily diet.

52. Lima Beans

Lima beans are slightly different from most beans you've had due to their buttery-like texture that adds a unique taste to any meal you're preparing. Lima beans are a terrific source of tryptophan, dietary fiber, manganese, folate, as well as potassium, and will even supply some iron to your diet as well. This makes them great for those who don't eat red meat to ensure that their nutritional requirements are met. Lima beans will really help to promote a healthier heart and will help you maintain higher energy levels without suffering from high's and low's.

53. Mangoes

One exotic fruit to make sure you consider adding to your diet plan is the mango. Mangoes contain 107 calories per cup and will provide you with 3 grams of fiber as well. This is another fruit that's rich in vitamin C so will help to boost your immune system and will also help to provide some antioxidant support as well due to its vitamin A content. Mangoes will help to satisfy your sweet tooth without throwing your diet off track.

54. Millet

Millet is one of the top gluten-free carb dense grains that you could be eating, so make sure you're putting it to use in your diet plan. Millet is rich in manganese, tryptophan, magnesium, as well as phosphorus and will contain 285 calories per one cup cooked. This grain will help to make sure your heart stays healthy by being a good source of magnesium as well as niacin and will help with the repair of damage tissue. After a hard workout session, this is a great carbohydrate to eat to restore muscle glycogen levels and help to promote protein synthesis.

55. Miso

Often known as an additive to soup, miso is high in tryptophan, manganese, vitamin K, zinc, copper, and contains a small amount of protein as well. You will want to check the ingredient label when purchasing miso however as while it's normally made from soybeans, in some cases it can be made from wheat, so if that's what's on the ingredient listing, you'll want to stay far, far away. Miso will help to promote a strong immune system and provide bone and blood vessel health support. Finally, soy has been shown to help protect against breast cancer, so females will want to pay special close attention to this food.

56. Mushrooms

Mushrooms earn top marks as a source of selenium as they provide over 50% of your total daily requirements in a 5 oz serving. In addition to that, they're also good sources of the B vitamins and are rich in copper, tryptophan, potassium, phosphorus, as well as zinc. Mushrooms will help to boost your overall immune system by making sure white blood cell production stays high and will also offer some clear anti-inflammatory benefits as well. Additionally, they may offer some anti-cancer benefits as well, noted by a study published in the African Journal of Biotechnology. This vegetable is one of the highest sources of protein amongst the vegetable family, so one vegetarians will want to be extra sure to take in.

57. Mustard Greens

Many cruciferous vegetables off cholesterol lowering benefits when steamed and mustard greens are no different. This food will be a potent source of vitamin K, vitamin A, as well as Vitamin C, amongst many more. Mustard greens contain phytonutrients and sulfur-containing nutrients that will also help with the detoxification process to remove waste by-products from the body. Finally, mustard greens can also help to bring down inflammation levels, which can put you at risk for cancer as well as many other chronic diseases.

58. Navy Beans

Another fiber all-star, navy beans are very high in folate, providing over 60% of your total daily requirements, so will be perfect for any pregnant women to be consuming. The high content of fiber in navy beans will also help to bring down your cholesterol levels as well and can reduce your risk of developing a heart attack as well. Navy beans will help to stabilize your blood glucose levels after you eat them, providing a slow release of energy as you go about your day. Finally, as they also provide a good dose of iron to your diet, navy beans can help ensure that you don't fatigue early when performing intense physical activity.

59. Olives

One food that's a great source of healthy fat that adds a unique flavor to many of your dishes is the olive. Whether you're eating green or black olives, this gluten-free food will provide a number of nutrients to your body that help to foster good health. Olives can help to treat high levels of inflammation in the body and also help to reduce the risk of cancer development as well. In addition to that, olives can also help to lower your levels of blood cholesterol and help to protect against heart disease. Add them to salads, on top of gluten-free pizza, or eat them on their own if you prefer.

60. Olive Oil

Containing similar benefits as the whole olive, olive oil is excellent for helping to promote heart health and is one big reason the people of the Mediterranean show such low rates of heart disease. Olive oil is one of the healthiest sources of fats that you could be eating and will add taste and moisture to many food dishes. Olive oil contains a high number of phytonutrients that will help to act as anti-inflammatories in the body as well as antioxidants. Finally, olive oil can also help to promote proper bone health as it can assist with the maintenance of higher levels of calcium in the body.

61. Onions

One nutrient that onions contain that is of particular interest is chromium, which can offer strong blood glucose control benefits. In addition to that, onions will also help to provide vitamin C, dietary fiber, manganese, as well as vitamin B6 to the body, along with folate, potassium, and phosphorus. Onions will help to boost heart health due to their sulfur-containing compounds that can help to provide anti-clotting effects. A regular consumption of onions may also help to decrease the levels of cholesterol in the body while lowering your triglycerides as well. Finally, onions may help to enhance the health of your connective tissues, allowing you to maintain strong bones and joints.

62. Oranges

Often known for their vitamin C content, oranges are great for strengthening the immune system and offering some dietary fiber as well. Oranges contain a number of phytonutrient compounds that will help to provide clear antioxidant benefits and help to protect against cancer. In addition to that, other diseases that oranges can help ward off due to their high antioxidant levels include asthma, osteoarthritis, as well as rheumatoid arthritis. Finally, oranges may help to lower the levels of bad cholesterol in the body, reducing your risk of heart disease.

63. Papaya

Papaya's are a wonderful fruit that contain a rich, buttery flavor that will provide a sweet treat at any point during the day. This seasonal fruit is extremely high in vitamin C with each papaya providing over 300% of your total daily requirements. In addition to that, papaya's are rich in folate, potassium, dietary fiber, vitamin A, vitamin E, as well as vitamin K. Papaya's are also going to protect against heart disease due to their high antioxidant concentration, as they are rich in vitamin A and vitamin E as well. These will all help to prevent the oxidation of cholesterol and improve your good to bad cholesterol ratio. Finally, papaya's will also help to boost your digestive health as well as warding off colon cancer.

64. Peanuts

Peanuts are another nut that packs in a good dose of healthy fats and has a taste that many people enjoy. Whether you choose to eat your peanuts whole or as peanut butter, they taste great on their own or alongside many different foods as well. Peanuts are a good source of manganese, tryptophan, as well as vitamin B3, folate and copper, and will provide a small amount of protein and fiber as well. Just be sure to eat your peanuts plain with no flavorings or seasonings as those could contain gluten that you need to be avoiding.

65. Pears

A sweet fruit that many people pass up for apples, pears are high in dietary fiber and will also provide you with some vitamin C, copper, as well as vitamin K as well. One pear has 97 calories so this is a fairly easy food to integrate into your total calorie intake. Pears will also help to protect against free radical damage taking place in the body while promoting strong cardiovascular and colon health. Finally, pears are one of the most hypoallergenic fruits available, so great for those who do have sensitive systems.

66. Peas

Sugar snap peas are the next great food to add into your diet. These taste delicious when added into a stir fry or salad, or can even be enjoyed straight on their own. Since you typically will eat the pod along with the peas, you'll get an extra dose of fiber as well. For anyone who enjoys the taste of regular green peas, these should definitely be on your menu.

67. Pineapple

While pineapples do rank in higher on the GI than some other fruits, that's no reason to exclude them from your diet plan. As long as you are sure to eat them in moderation and preferably with a protein source, they won't have too great of a response on your blood sugar levels. Pineapples are also a good source of manganese, vitamin C, vitamin B1, as well as copper and will help to reduce the level of inflammation in the body. Pineapples can also assist with the digestion process due to a compound called bromelain, which is found in the pineapple.

68. Pinto Beans

To boost your daily fiber intake, turn to pinto beans which will help you achieve this in a flash. Pinto beans are also rich in folate, tryptophan, manganese, protein, phosphorus, as well as iron, magnesium, and potassium. Pinto beans are rich in complex carbohydrates so great for those days when you are especially active and need more energy. They will easily take the replacement of higher calorie wheat-derived products in your diet to sustain the energy that you need. Pinto beans can also help to lower your overall risk of heart attack and stabilize your blood glucose levels.

69. Plums

A small fruit that contains just 36 calories per piece is the plum. This fruit packs in vitamin C, vitamin A, as well as fiber, and will also provide you with some vitamin B2 as well. Plums contain phenols, which can help to protect you against free radical damage in the body and also help you absorb iron in your diet better as well. For anyone who is suffering from iron deficiency anemia, this is a terrific food to have in your diet. Finally, plums can also help to support healthy eyes as they will help to protect against macular degeneration.

70. Pork

One lean source of protein that is often overlooked is pork. While there are fattier cuts of pork available, as long as you choose one that has less visible fat and no marbling of fat, you will be getting a quality source of protein that will help with muscle tissue building and repair. Pork is rich in vitamin C, Niacin, phosphorus, as well as Zinc, which is especially important for helping with the process of building lean muscle mass. In addition to that, it will provide you with some iron as well, so for anyone who struggles to get in enough iron on their diet due to a low beef consumption, pork is a great type of meat to consume.

71. Potatoes

Potatoes are one food that anyone on a gluten-free diet will definitely want to be making good use of. Potatoes can be prepared in a number of different ways and if you don't prepare them with butter, they'll definitely rate in as being a very low fat food. Potatoes contain a good dose of vitamin C, vitamin B6, copper, as well as potassium, so will help support high physical activity levels. In addition to that, potatoes contain a high level of phytochemicals, coming close to broccoli. This helps them protect you from cancer as well as cardiovascular disease. Consuming potatoes on a regular basis can also help you lower your blood pressure as well, so are a great addition for anyone suffering from this health concern.

72. Pumpkin Seeds

In the quest to get healthy fats in your diet plan, don't overlook pumpkin seeds. Pumpkin seeds have a unique flavor and work great topped over a salad or added to trail mix. Pumpkin seeds are a good source of manganese, magnesium, phosphorus, tryptophan, as well as iron, and will also supply you with small doses of zinc, vitamin K, and protein as well. Pumpkin seeds are especially important for the male to consider as they can help to improve prostate health due to the type of oil that they contain. In addition to this, the Zinc content in pumpkin seeds also helps to support proper male reproductive health. Finally, the monounsaturated fat in pumpkin seeds will also help to reduce inflammation in the body and keep your heart health.

73. Quinoa

Quinoa is the next grain to consider to help you meet your complex carbohydrate needs and maintain higher energy levels. It's high in manganese, magnesium, as well as iron and tryptophan, and will also supply you with a complete source of protein. This is especially important for anyone to consider who's following a vegetarian diet plan as most vegetarians aren't getting enough high quality protein sources in their daily diet. Quinoa also offers good support for those who suffer from migraines on a regular basis due to the combination of magnesium as well as riboflavin it contains. Add quinoa into any dish as you would rice and you'll welcome this slight change.

74. Raisins

If you're looking for an energy dense food to turn to in order to power you through your day, raisins make for a great pick. Raisins are very high in carbohydrates and will keep your blood sugar levels elevated for times of intense physical activity. Since raisins are dried grapes, they'll contain the phenols that grapes will, helping to protect you from free radical damage. In addition to that, they're also a good source of boron, which can help to strengthen the bones, especially when menopause sets in for women. Finally, raisins provide support to fight macular degeneration, so will help keep your eyes in top shape as well.

75. Raspberries

One of the fruits that contains the lowest amount of sugar that you'll want to snack on is raspberries. This tart berry is rich in manganese, vitamin C, and also packs in a high dose of fiber as well, making it an excellent fruit as far as appetite control goes. Raspberries are also high in folate, vitamin B2, magnesium, as well as potassium, so will help to keep your muscles energized. Raspberries are rich in phytonutrients that provide both antioxidant as well as anti-microbial protection, reducing the chances that you suffer from certain bacteria and fungi infections.

76. Rice

Rice is a great gluten-free food to add in replacement of pasta in many of the meals that you eat on your diet plan. If you choose to eat brown rice, you'll take in many of the nutritional components of natural rice as the preparation process only removes the layer of the hull that is directly on the outside. The top nutrients that rice is rich in include manganese, selenium, magnesium, as well as tryptophan. The manganese in rice is going to work as a strong antioxidant in the body and will help to protect against free radical damage. In addition to this, the fiber and selenium in brown rice can help to lower your risk of colon cancer, so if that disease is a concern of yours, this is one must-have food.

77. Rice Flour

Another gluten-free alternative to regular flour that you might consider using is rice flour. Rice flour contains very little fat while being high in carbohydrates and is likewise a good source of manganese as well. While you cannot use rice flour as a direct substitute in all the recipes that you're preparing, it does often work well with most dishes.

78. Romaine Lettuce

If you're typically preparing your salads with iceberg lettuce, it's definitely time for you to change this. While salads themselves can generally be quite low in calories and healthy to eat, if you're using the wrong mix of ingredients, they'll be anything but. Romaine lettuce packs far more nutrients than iceberg does and contains the same number of calories. At just 15 per two cup serving, you definitely can add this into your diet plan. Romaine lettuce is high in vitamin K, vitamin A, vitamin C, as well as folate, manganese, chromium, potassium, iron, vitamin B2, phosphorus, calcium, and even contains a very small amount of omega 3 fatty acids. Romaine lettuce's folic acid content can help to convert homocysteine into another less harmful substances, also reducing your risk of suffering from heart attacks and strokes.

79. Salmon

One of the healthiest sources of fish to consume in your diet plan is salmon. Salmon is loaded with omega-3 fatty acids and will help to promote a healthy brain while managing your blood glucose levels. A regular intake of salmon in the diet can help to increase insulin sensitivity, which will then help you manage the carbohydrates that you consume better. Some of the primary nutrients that salmon is high in include tryptophan, vitamin D, omega fatty acids, selenium, protein, vitamin B3, vitamin B12, phosphorus, as well as magnesium. The omega-3 fats in salmon will also help to stabilize your mood and can enhance your cognition and concentration levels as well.

80. Sardines

Moving along, the next food to include in your diet plan is sardines. Sardines are likewise rich in omega-3 fatty acids and are going to help to support a healthy mind as well. They're also a great source of vitamin B12, selenium, vitamin D, phosphorus, as well as calcium, and contain 191 calories per 3.25 oz. serving. Sardines will support strong bones due to the calcium as well as vitamin D content and will allow you to meet your daily protein requirements with ease. Most people shun sardines because they think they taste less than ideal, but don't be afraid to experiment with them and find a way to consume them that you enjoy. If prepared in a new manner, you may just find that you really do enjoy the taste they have to offer.

81. Scallops

Scallops are the next type of seafood to discuss adding to your gluten-free diet. Scallops are very rich in protein and contain very little fat, with the fat that they do contain coming from omega-3 fatty acids. Scallops are also rich in tryptophan, vitamin B12, phosphorus, as well as magnesium and potassium, so will go a long way towards promoting strong muscular contractions. Scallops will help to support strong cardiovascular health as they help to keep homocysteine levels low and will ensure that the blood vessels leading to and from the heart are contracting and relaxing as they should be. Finally, scallops can help to protect against you against heart arrhythmia and help you maintain a more natural heart rhythm.

82. Sesame Seeds

Sesame seeds offer a fresh nutty taste to your dishes and can work great in salads, baked goods, or even sprinkled on top of a stir-fry. Sesame seeds are rich in healthy fat content and contain a good dose of copper, manganese, tryptophan, calcium, magnesium, as well as iron, which is something that many people are not getting enough of. Sesame seeds can help to protect against rheumatoid arthritis and will provide support to your respiratory system as well. They can help to reduce the symptoms associated with asthma, lower your risk of heart attack, stroke, and heart disease, as well as prevent migraines in those individuals who are prone to experiencing these. Finally, sesame seeds are also good for restoring normal sleep patterns in women with menopause who are struggling to sleep soundly.

83. Shrimp

The next low calorie seafood to consider adding to your diet is shrimp. Shrimp is often served as a special treat as it is slightly higher in price than some other protein sources but does offer numerous nutritional benefits so you should consider adding it a little more often. Shrimp is high in tryptophan, selenium, protein, vitamin D, vitamin B12 iron, as well as phosphorus, and will supply you with a small amount of omega-3 fatty acids as well. Shrimp is very good for promoting heart health despite being high in cholesterol as it helps to increase the levels of good cholesterol in the body more than it raises the levels of bad cholesterol. Therefore, the overall effect is positive as far as your health is concerned. Finally, shrimp will also help to control high blood pressure and prevent the risk of heart disease.

84. Spinach

One must-have green vegetable in your diet plan is spinach. Spinach is one of the top nutritional sources to add into your salad as it's very good for decreasing the risk of cancer, especially of the prostate. Spinach is rich in vitamin K, vitamin A, manganese, folate, magnesium, iron, vitamin C, as well as the B vitamins and is also high in calcium as well. Along with its cancer protection benefits, spinach can also help to reduce the level of inflammation in the body, putting you in an overall healthier state, as noted by the Journal of Mercian College of Cardiology. Finally, the vitamin K found in spinach, which accounts for almost 200% of your total daily requirement can help to increase the density and strength of the bones, reducing your risk of stress fractures or osteoporosis.

85. Strawberries

One of the sweetest berries that many people like to enjoy, strawberries are a terrific gluten-free food to add into your diet program. Strawberries are high in vitamin C content, providing well over 136% of your total requirements and are also a good source of manganese as well. In addition to this, they'll supply you with a small amount of dietary fiber as well as iodine. Potassium, folate, vitamin B6 vitamin B5, and vitamin B6 are also nutrients that you'll take in when you serve these up as a quick snack or for dessert. They'll help to keep your cardiovascular system healthy, stabilize your blood glucose levels, while also helping to provide anti-inflammatory effects to the body as well.

86. Soy Flour

Soy flour is another great alternative to regular wheat derived flour for those who suffer from gluten intolerance to include in their diet plan. Soy flour is rich in protein, which cannot be said for regular flour and is also high in iron, B vitamins, and calcium. While there has been quite a bit of controversy surrounding soy based products, much research does show that it can reduce the risk of heart disease, so is a good food to consider adding to your diet plan. Soy flour can also help to reduce the symptoms that are associated with menopause as well such as hot flashes, night sweats, irritability, and mood swings.

87. Soybeans

Another soy based food to consider adding to your diet plan is the soybean. Soybeans are high in tryptophan, manganese, protein, as well as iron, and will also supply you with some omega-3 fatty acids as well. Soybeans are a good source of phosphorus and dietary fiber and will even offer some vitamin K and magnesium as well. Soy beans are a great gluten-free food for vegetarians to be eating due to the fact that they are high in protein content and they can also help promote a leaner body as well. Soy based foods can assist with the lowering of blood pressure as well as cholesterol in addition to that, so if those are two important health effects you're looking for, you'll definitely want to take note of that benefit.

88. Squash

Squash, which comes in both summer and winter varieties, is an excellent vegetable to add into your diet plan. Many people who crave pasta but who want to sustain a gluten-free diet will benefit from using spaghetti squash in their diet, which his lower in calories than traditional pasta and packs more of a nutrient punch. Squash is also high in manganese, vitamin C, magnesium, vitamin A, potassium, along with many of the B vitamins. Squash will provide strong antioxidant and anti-inflammatory benefits and works great for those with diabetes or who are concerned about blood sugar management as it will help to stabilize the blood glucose levels very well.

89. Sunflower seeds

Sunflower seeds are another terrific seed to add into your diet plan that are going to bring about good health benefits and help keep your hunger level down. This gluten-free food is high in vitamin E, vitamin B1, manganese, magnesium, copper, tryptophan, selenium, as well as phosphorus and contains 205 calories per quarter cup serving. Sunflower seeds are going to provide strong anti-inflammatory benefits to the body and will also help to reduce the risk of colon cancer as well. They contain phytosterols that will lower cholesterol levels and promote good heart health.

90. Swiss Chard

Swiss chard is a green vegetable that often gets overlooked in the diets of many yet should be included more regularly. Swiss chard is high in vitamin K and A, offering well over 100% of your total daily requirements. In addition to that, it's also high in vitamin C, magnesium, manganese, potassium, and iron, and will supply you with many B vitamins as well. This food is great for helping to regulate your blood glucose levels and supporting strong bones.

91. Sweet Potato

While potatoes are a great gluten-free food to include in your diet plan, even better is the sweet potato. Sweet potatoes rank in lower on the GI scale so will have lesser of an impact on your blood glucose level. In addition to that, sweet potatoes will provide up to 90% of your total daily vitamin A needs and also give you a good dose of vitamin C as well. Sweet potatoes are rich in manganese and copper and will provide enough fiber to keep your hunger levels low after eating them.

92. Tofu

For vegetarians on a gluten free diet plan, tofu is a must-turn to food as it will help you maintain a high enough protein intake needed to maintain your lean mass tissue. Tofu is not only going to provide protein though, it also packs in some essential fatty acids, selenium, as well as calcium, which is needed to support strong bones, especially in postmenopausal women, as noted in a study published in the American Society for Nutrition. Regularly consuming tofu in your diet can also help to maintain your cardiovascular system and help to decrease the symptoms associated with menopause in those who are suffering.

93. Tomatoes

One food that earns top marks for the antioxidant content it contains are tomatoes. Tomatoes are very rich in lycopene, which is especially important for males as it will help to promote better prostate health. Tomatoes are also very high in vitamin C content and will provide you with a good dose of vitamin A and vitamin K as well. Furthermore, they're good for the B vitamins, which are necessary to sustain high energy levels throughout the day. Finally, the lycopene found in tomatoes can also enhance your bone health, so that's yet another reason to consider adding these to your day.

94. Tuna

Tuna is another excellent protein source that comes from the sea that provides your body with wonderful nutritional benefits. High in selenium and protein, this fish is going to help to keep your brain healthy, improve your cholesterol profile, and increase your heart rate variability, which is a measure of heart function. Finally, tuna can also help to prevent and control high blood pressure, so is important for those battling this condition.

95. Turkey

Often only eaten on special occasions, consider adding turkey more often into your regular diet plan. As long as you choose the white meat varieties, which do contain far less fat than dark meat, turkey is a terrific source of protein that will also provide you with tryptophan, selenium, vitamin B3, vitamin B6, phosphorus, and zinc. Turkey will help to promote proper muscle tissue rebuilding after a hard workout, so is great for those involved in intense workout programs.

96. Turnip Greens

If you want to increase your intake of vitamin K, look no further than to turnip greens. This food provides over 600% of your daily requirement for this nutrient and is also a great source of vitamin A, C, E, and the B vitamins. In addition to that, it also offers up some folate, so is a great food for pregnant women to be consuming. Turnip greens can help to assist with the detoxification process in the body, ensuring you feel well at all times.

97. Venison

One great alternative to beef to help meet your protein and iron requirements is venison. Venison is very high in vitamin B12, vitamin B2, vitamin B3, and phosphorus, and will help to enhance your metabolic rate. Since venison is a great source of riboflavin in the body, and this nutrient is needed for energy production, this is a good protein source to have before or after a workout.

98. Walnuts

One of the nut variations that's high in omega fats that you should be eating regularly is walnuts. Walnuts are going to help to decrease your risk of insulin resistance while providing strong heart-health benefits. In addition to that, they're high in vitamin E content as well, which will help to protect you from free radical damage and provide strong antioxidant activity as noted in a study published by the University of Texas Health Science Center.

99. Watermelon

If you need a sweet, low calorie treat, consider watermelon. At just 48 calories per one cup serving, this fruit is the perfect addition to any gluten-free diet and will provide you with some vitamin A as well as vitamin C. It's also a good source of vitamin B6, vitamin B1, and will contain some potassium to promote strong muscle contractions as well. Watermelon is also high in lycopene, which can be very powerful for reducing the risk of cancer.

100. Yams

Another food similar to the sweet potato is the yam. Yams are rich in vitamin C content, contain some potassium, and also provide you with over a quarter of your daily needs for fiber per one cup serving. At 157 calories per cup, these are also lower than rice or pasta as well. Yams will help to protect against cardiovascular disease due to the vitamin B6 content it has and will also help to promote blood sugar control as well.

101. Zucchini

Zucchini is a great food to eat in many different ways. Add them to salads, added to a stir-fry, or baked and served as a side dish. Zucchini is a low calorie food at just 36 calories per cup and is high in manganese, vitamin C, magnesium, vitamin A, as well as potassium. Zucchini will help to provide antioxidant benefits in the body, regulate your blood sugar, and help to decrease your overall level of inflammation present as well. This can then reduce other diseases such as diabetes and arthritis.

Handy List for Shopping for
the 101 Best Gluten-Free Foods

Below you will find the foods listed in a section where you might find them in a grocery store. Some items may be found in more than one place in your store so that is why you will find them listed in more than one section below. Whenever possible … eat FRESH … not canned or preserved. Enjoy!

PRODUCE

Apples
Apricots
Asparagus
Avocados
Bananas
Beets
Bell peppers
Blackberries
Blueberries Corn
Cucumbers
Eggplant
Fennel
Figs
Garlic
Grapefruit
Grapes
Green Beans
Green Peas
Kale
Kiwifruit
Leeks
Lemons
Mangoes
Mushrooms
Mustard Greens
Onions
Oranges
Papaya
Pears
Peas
Pineapple
Plums
Potatoes
Raspberries
Romaine Lettuce
Spinach
Strawberries
Squash
Swiss Chard

Sweet Potato
Tomatoes
Turnip Greens
Watermelon
Yams
Zucchini

LENTILS/GRAINS
Black Beans
Buckwheat
Chick Peas
Flaxseeds
Kidney Beans
Lentils
Lima Beans
Millet
Navy Beans
Pinto Beans
Quinoa
Rice
Soybeans

MEATS
Beef
Chicken
Cod
Halibut
Pork
Salmon
Sardines
Scallops
Shrimp

Tuna
Turkey
Venison

DAIRY
Cheese
Greek yogurt
Tofu

NUTS/SEEDS
Almonds
Cashew
Peanuts
Pumpkin Seeds
Sesame Seeds
Sunflower Seeds
Walnuts

DRINKS
Coffee
Green Tea

STAPLES/MISC.
Almond Butter
Almond Flour
Corn Meal
Miso
Olives
Olive Oil
Rice Flour
Soy Flour
Raisins

Celiac Disease Awareness Campaign
Of The National Institutes of Health

Traveling With Celiac Disease

If you like to travel, celiac disease doesn't need to be a roadblock. With some planning, you can eat safely when traveling by land, sea, or air and maintain a gluten-free diet once you reach your destination, according to celiac disease experts. Here's what they suggest:

Do some research.

Find out if the hotel, bed and breakfast, or resort where you will stay offers gluten-free food. If you have a choice of accommodations, choose a place that caters to special dietary needs or has a kitchenette that will allow you to store and prepare food. Even a microwave or small refrigerator is helpful, especially if you are traveling with children who are on a gluten-free diet.

Before you leave, try to find out if the city or area you will be traveling to has a celiac support group or organization, which could be a great source of information about local places to stay, eat, and shop for food. Or, if you are part of a celiac support group or organization at home—or have friends with celiac disease or gluten intolerance—check with them before you begin making travel plans. Someone from home who has been where you are going may have invaluable advice.

Before your trip, you also can search online for gluten-free restaurants by city, state, type of cuisine, or restaurant chain through a program run by the Gluten Intolerance Group of North America (GIG). The Gluten-Free Restaurant Awareness Program (GFRAP) currently lists close to 900 U.S. restaurants that offer gluten-free menu options, and the list is growing, according to GFRAP Manager Madelyn Smith.

Plan ahead.

If possible, pack food to bring with you when you travel. Good choices include a jar of peanut butter, a foil pack of tuna fish, or some gluten-free crackers or pretzels, according to Anne Roland Lee, MSEd, RD, a nutritionist with Columbia University's Celiac Disease Center. Even if you think you won't need it, delays or other unforeseen events could arise, leaving you hungry and without access to gluten-free food.

Roger Elliott, founder of celiactravel.com, recommends carrying at least one meal's worth of calories with you. "If you don't, you'll find yourself hungry and taking risks you wouldn't otherwise take," he said.

Depending on how you are traveling, you also might want to consider the following:

- **By air**: Request a gluten-free meal in advance and remind the flight attendant about it once you board the plane. It's also a good idea to double check with your server before you eat. If for some reason your pre-ordered meal doesn't arrive or gets contaminated with gluten-containing food, you'll have the food you packed. Good snacks to bring to the airport include gluten-free rice cakes, corn chips, nuts, and dried or fresh fruit. If you find out the airline does not prepare gluten-free meals, eat before you travel or bring a sandwich or more substantial snack to eat at the airport or on the plane. If you are traveling internationally, avoid packing large amounts of gluten-free food in case customs makes you leave it behind.

- **By sea**: Work with the human resources staff of the cruise line you will be using to order your gluten-free meals in advance. Be sure to follow up right before your trip and again when you board ship. Nearly all cruise lines can now accommodate people with gluten intolerance, according to Smith, who has celiac disease.

- **By land**: If you are driving or taking a train, bring gluten-free crackers, cookies, and other snacks, or meal supplements such as bread. You also can bring a cooler and pack perishable, gluten-free items such as meat, cheese, and yogurt, recommends Smith. You might want to invest in a cooler that plugs into the car and does not require ice, she said. You can plug the cooler in once you get to a hotel room so you will have enough food for the duration of your stay.

Follow through.

Once you reach your destination, follow the same guidelines you did while traveling. Call ahead to restaurants with your request for a gluten-free meal, and confirm it once you arrive and again before you eat.

Ethnic restaurants might be a good option because they often serve foods, such as black beans and rice or pad thai, that are naturally gluten-free, healthy, and tasty, said Lee. If you don't like ethnic food, Lee recommends an old standby: steak—grilled plain with nothing added—and a baked potato.

Another approach is to hand your server a restaurant card explaining celiac disease and its necessary dietary restrictions. With the cards, you don't have to rely on servers to remember to convey your information to the chef or to understand what you said. Elliott, who has celiac disease and likes to travel, created restaurant cards in 38 languages to help people like himself.

If you can prepare food where you are staying, go grocery shopping. Be careful when checking nutrition labels if you are in another country—different countries have different rules about food labeling. If you are used to gluten-free bread and other baked-good mixes, you might want to bring some from home in case you can't find them at your destination. Another useful item to bring, according to Smith, is a special bag made to cook food in the toaster oven or microwave to prevent cross contamination from gluten-containing breadcrumbs.

Stick with it.

Finally, stick with your diet. Staying gluten-free and healthy will help you enjoy your vacation and your travels.

Gluten-Free Restaurant Awareness Program Helps Travelers

The Gluten Intolerance Group of North America (GIG) is helping individually and corporately owned U.S. restaurants understand the dietary needs of people with gluten intolerance through the Gluten- Free Restaurant Awareness Program (GFRAP).

Interested restaurants can participate in the program on three different levels, according to GFRAP Manager Madelyn Smith. The first level offers restaurant owners a basic packet of education and training materials, along with a review of their gluten-free menus and assistance from a program resource person. The second level includes an intensive menu review of recipes and ingredients by qualified nutrition experts in addition to the education and training materials. The third level offers a comprehensive restaurant training program in addition to the packet of materials and menu review offered in levels one and two.

Participating restaurants pay for the training. The cost of the program depends on the level of participation a restaurant chooses.

The GFRAP began as an initiative of the Westchester, NY, Celiac Sprue Support Group. The GIG assumed operation of the expanding program and combined it with the GIG's Corporate Restaurant Program last July, according to Smith. "This program is great for travelers because they can search for a restaurant by city, state, or cuisine," she said. "Our vision is for the program to become international."

Websites

Celiac Disease Center at Columbia University
www.celiacdiseasecenter.columbia.edu

Celiac Travel www.celiactravel.com

Gluten-Free Restaurant Awareness Program www.glutenfreerestaurants.org

Gluten Intolerance Group of North America www.gluten.net

To meet the need for comprehensive and current information about celiac disease, the National Digestive Diseases Information Clearinghouse, a service of the National Institute of Diabetes and Digestive and Kidney Diseases (NIDDK), launched the Celiac Disease Awareness Campaign. The Awareness Campaign is the result of the combined ideas and efforts of the professional and voluntary organizations that focus on celiac disease, along with the NIDDK, the National Institutes of Health, and the Centers for Disease Control and Prevention. Visit www.celiac.nih.gov to learn more about the Awareness Campaign.

Celiac Disease Awareness Campaign

c/o National Digestive Diseases Information Clearinghouse

2 Information Way

Bethesda, MD 20892–3570

Phone: 1–800–891–5389

TTY: 1–866–569–1162

Fax: 703–738–4929

Email: celiac@info.niddk.nih.gov

Internet: www.celiac.nih.gov